As you read this book you will be able to find the answers to many
questions about yourself and the way you do things. This book
is based on part of the popular 'Living and Working Together' exhibition
at **EUREKA! The Museum for Children** in Halifax. **EUREKA!** is
the first museum in Great Britain designed especially for children.
The Museum's exhibitions use an exciting new approach, placing the
child at the centre of learning, and the book has been designed to
bring the best of the exhibition into your home or classroom.

The book is full of activities and information. It offers plenty of talking
points for children and adults and shows how learning together can
be fun. The book will appeal to the child in us all.

EUREKA! The Museum for Children 1995

My name is Socrates. I live
at EUREKA! Help me to
find out all there is to know
about the world in which
you live and work.

ACKNOWLEDGEMENTS

Riverswift would like to thank the staff of Bounds Green Junior School in London,
of Warley Road Primary School in Halifax and all the children
who appear in the photographs.

Models from EUREKA! and exhibition design by Tim Hunkin,
Satoshi Kitamura and Greville White
Photography by Jenny Matthews and Katie Vandyck
Design by Mandy Sherliker

First published 1995

1 3 5 7 9 10 8 6 4 2

First published in the United Kingdom in 1995 by
Riverswift
Random House, 20 Vauxhall Bridge Road, London SW1V 2SA

Random House Australia (Pty) Limited
20 Alfred Street, Milsons Point, Sydney,
New South Wales 2061, Australia

Random House New Zealand Limited
18 Poland Road, Glenfield
Auckland 10, New Zealand

Random House South Africa (Pty) Limited
PO Box 337, Bergvlei, South Africa

Random House UK Limited Reg. No. 954009

The EUREKA! series of books is based on the displays at
EUREKA! The Museum for Children, Discovery Road, Halifax,
Yorkshire, England, HX1 2NE. Tel: 0422 330069

A CIP Catalogue record for this book is
available from the British Library

ISBN 1 898304 71 8

Printed in Italy by Grafiche AZ Verona

Living and Working Together

A **EUREKA!**™ Book

Brenda Walpole

Illustrations by Satoshi Kitamura

RIVERSWIFT

LONDON

Off I go!

Hello! My name is Socrates, and I want to know all about what you get up to when you go out. My life is very simple. I eat and sleep and stroll about. But your lives seem much more complicated.

This is the town square at EUREKA!

Your home is a place where you can see your family, sleep, have meals and play, but you don't stay there all the time. You go out to the village street or the town centre for all sorts of reasons.

For a start, most people have to go to the shops to buy food before they can eat. They go out to buy other things too, everything from soap to sticky tape. You go out to school. Most grown-ups go out to work, and just about everyone goes out to enjoy themselves. A town centre is a busy place, where people work, shop and meet their friends.

Socrates investigates

Note it down
Make a note of each time you go out and where you go in one week.

Make
Make a model of a desert island with just a few people living on it. Imagine the outings they might have.

Write
Write about how you would live if there were no shops today.

Hmmm . . . It sounds exciting out there.

How do I get my food?

People feed me. My food usually comes from a tin or a packet. Sometimes I hunt for mice or birds, but I've never seen you go hunting. Where do you find your food?

Long ago, your ancestors hunted wild animals to eat and picked fruit and nuts from the trees. Then they kept their own animals and grew their own crops. They went to a market if they wanted to buy or sell anything. You can still buy food at a market or a supermarket, or your local shops. Markets are busy, bustling places.

Everything is laid out on stalls for you to see. You might buy just the amount of fresh fruit or vegetables that you need for that day. The stallholder weighs the goods and puts them in a bag for you. It's different at the supermarket. There are hundreds of packets and cans along the neat and tidy shelves. You choose from a selection that has come from all over the world.

You can use a trolley and buy all the food you need for a week at once. The shop assistant uses a scanner to read the barcodes on each item so the electronic cash register can add everything up.

Socrates investigates

Write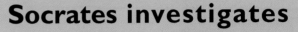

Imagine a day in the life of a supermarket trolley. Write about the adventures it might have.

Make ✂

Make a shop or market stall of your own. What will it sell? How will you show when your shop is open? Make some pretend money to use at your shop.

> Working in a food shop sounds just the sort of job for me!

Where does my food come from?

I know where mice live and I catch them if I can. But where do your bananas and eggs, frozen pizzas and baked beans come from?

Farmers all over the world grow grain and vegetables and fruit. Other farmers keep the animals that give us milk and cheese and eggs and meat. One farm provides enough food for lots of people. Some farm products are taken on to factories to be mixed, chopped, cooked and packaged.

Wheat is harvested and taken to the mill where it is ground into flour. At the bakery, flour is mixed with yeast, water and other ingredients to make bread and pizzas and biscuits. Fresh milk is collected from cows every day. Tankers take it to the dairy where it is poured into bottles or cartons. Some vegetables and fruits are frozen or canned so that they will stay fresh for a long time.

Big lorries and vans take the food from the farms to the factories and warehouses and shops. Can you think of some foods which travel a long way before you eat them? Some are brought by sea and air.

Socrates investigates

Experiment

Grow your own food! Put some damp cotton wool on a saucer. Sprinkle cress seeds all over it. Water them a little each day. When the seeds have grown you can cut the cress and eat it with egg or cheese in a sandwich.

Note it down

Look at food labels to find which countries they come from. Where did your tea, orange juice and pasta come from?

Farmers, lorry drivers, factory operators . . .
I see now that it takes a lot of people and a lot of work to get my food into its tin.

Where are things made?

> I don't need clothes. Nor do I need cleaning materials, toys, computers or cars or any of the other things that humans seem to want. Where do they all come from? Who makes them?

Take a look around the room you are in at the moment. You will probably see a table, a chair, books, perhaps a TV or a computer, a carpet. All these things have been made in workshops and factories, then taken to shops for people to buy.

Small workshops may have only five or six people working in them, but factories can have hundreds. People usually work in teams where everyone has a special job. These children are making containers on a factory production line at EUREKA! One operator presses out the shape, the next one puts on the handles and the last one prints a pattern on the outside. Everyone on the production line must work at the same speed. What would happen if they didn't? Machines can be noisy, dangerous and hot. If you work near one, you need overalls and special clothes to protect your ears, eyes or hands.

At EUREKA! children can dress up in all sorts of different work clothes.

Socrates investigates

Draw

Draw yourself in the clothes you would wear in a car factory.

Experiment

With some friends, pretend to work on a factory production line making toy dinosaurs. The first operator could roll modelling clay flat and the second could cut out shapes. What else would need to be done?

I suppose lots of people have jobs operating machines and making things.

How do I pay?

I know that you go to the bank sometimes to get money. I've even seen people getting money from a hole in the wall! Is the bank a shop, too? Does it give the money away?

When people are buying something expensive, they sometimes pay by cheque. The words and numbers they write on the cheque tell their bank to pay that sum of money into the shop's bank.

You have to have money in the bank before you can take it out. Most people who go out to work are paid at the end of each week or month. They put the money in a bank to keep it safe. Then they can take the money out when they need it.

Banks keep the money in strong safes and vaults with locked doors. They use burglar alarms and video cameras to stop people breaking in to steal it.

Cash machines outside the bank have money inside them. You have to use your cash card and key in your own number before any money will come out. The bank's computer works out how much money you have left.

Socrates investigates

Make

Put a coin under a sheet of white paper and rub over it with a crayon or soft pencil. You will have a copy of the picture on the coin. Make rubbings of different coins. What pictures do they have on them?

Draw

Different countries have different pictures on their bank notes. Make up your own paper money. America has dollars, France has francs and Britain has pounds. What will you name your money?

> I prefer a life without money - but then I'm lucky to have everything I need!

Learning and finding out

When I was a kitten my mother taught me how to hunt - stalking, chasing, pouncing, and so on. But you have so many different things to learn - how to turn things on and off, make things, buy things, read and write. Where do you learn to do all this?

You go out to work every day too! You do school work, and sometimes it's quite hard. In some lessons you learn skills that might be useful when you have a job - like adding up and cutting out, drawing, playing music and sport. But all the things you learn at school help you to understand the world better when you grow up. It's the teacher's job to help you learn. You can also find out information for yourself from books and computers. With lots of practice you can improve your skills at almost anything. A school is an important part of a village or town. Everyone knows where it is.

Parents as well as children and teachers meet there. In big cities schools are very good places for families to get to know each other.

Socrates investigates

Note it down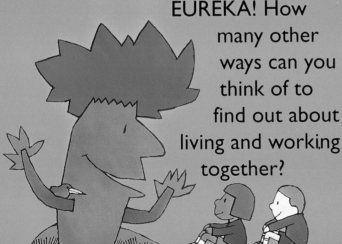
You are reading this book to find out about how people live and work. You could also learn from watching a video or visiting EUREKA! How many other ways can you think of to find out about living and working together?

Draw
Imagine you had to explain to someone how to work a television or start a video without using words. Draw a set of pictures to tell them what to do.

So that's why you go off to school each day!

How do people help each other?

I can see why a school is an important part of a town - it's where the children go! What other places are important to the town? Who looks after people who can't work or look after themselves?

Hospitals, community centres, churches and temples are also important to a town. A hospital is where you go if you are ill. There are special homes where you can be looked after if you can't manage on your own. Big buildings are needed for some of the things people do together. Churches, temples mosques and synagogues are places where people meet to pray. Members meet to celebrate happy events like the birth of a new baby. They take care of each other when things go wrong or if someone dies.

People who belong to local clubs some-times raise money to help others with a sponsored swim or a concert.

Socrates investigates

Make

Dress up and pretend to be someone who helps others. You could be a doctor, a nurse, or a priest or a teacher. How do they help people?

Write

Write about something you have done to help others.

I hope some of you will become vets when you grow up, so you can take care of me!

Keeping the rules

I've heard an ambulance rushing to hospital. I've heard police cars and fire engines too. Are the police station and the fire station important places?

Lots of people have jobs which help to keep us all safe. Lollipop ladies and men, lifeguards and firefighters are just a few. Life in the town is safer if everyone follows a few rules.

If there is a car crash, firefighters try to stop the cars catching fire. The ambulance crew take injured people to hospital. The police try to find out what happened and whose fault the crash was.

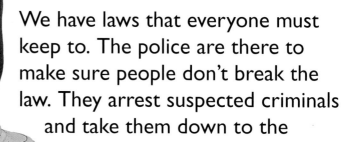

We have laws that everyone must keep to. The police are there to make sure people don't break the law. They arrest suspected criminals and take them down to the

police station. A law court with a judge and jury or a magistrate decides who should be punished.

Socrates investigates

What rules do you have at school to keep children safe?
Who makes sure that everyone keeps to the rules?

Note it down
When you go out in a car see how many different road signs you can spot. Look for the signs that

mean "no entry", "roadworks" or "school near by".

I must try not to steal scraps from the dustbin next door . . . I'm glad there are rules about cars because they are very dangerous.

How do I get about?

When I go near the road I keep well away from cars and buses but my family travel in them all the time. I need to know more about who drives them and who looks after them.

There's lots of traffic in a busy town centre. People drive their own cars to work or to the shops. They park them in car parks or at the side of the road.

Some people prefer to go on the bus so they don't have to do the driving. Buses go from one side of town to the other, picking people up and letting them off on the way.

Lorries carry goods all across the country from factories and warehouses to shops.
Cars and buses and lorries have to be filled up with fuel at the filling station.
They go to the garage to be fixed by garage mechanics. The mechanics

lift the car up on a ramp so they can look underneath. Cars can take us quickly from one place to another, but they can be noisy and smelly. What do you think is the best way to get about town?

Socrates investigates

Draw
Design a traffic system for an ideal town. How would it work if people could only use bicycles?

Talk
Ask the older people in your family how they travelled to school. How long did it take them?

I'd rather stay close to home than travel in those things.

Going out and having fun

I only go out when I need to. I prefer to curl up and sleep. Are there places you can go to just enjoy yourself? Does anybody work there?

In bigger towns there is a cinema and a theatre and a museum and all sorts of cafés, restaurants and snack bars.

Most towns have at least one park, and there's usually a swimming pool or a sports centre near by.

Lots of people have jobs in these places. Park attendants look after the park. There are lifeguards and swimming instructors at the pool and trainers at the sports centre. There are ushers and usherettes at the cinema, actors at the theatre and a curator at the museum. Cooks make the food in restaurants and waiters serve it. Can you think of some other people who work at the places where we have fun?

Socrates investigates

Write

Many people have jobs looking after the places we visit. Imagine your job is guarding and cleaning the dinosaurs in a museum. Write about what you would do.

Make ✂

Actors at the theatre entertain hundreds of people every day. Make your own play. Dress up and act out a story with some of your friends or use puppets to put on a show.

I wouldn't mind working at a fish restaurant . . .

How a town grows

I'm happy in my home. I don't need any more space to live. But people seem to spend ages mending their homes and building more houses and roads.

Villages grow into towns, and towns can become cities as more people move to live and work in them. Everybody needs a home so new ones have to be built. The people need shops, offices, factories, schools and roads too.

Think of all the different jobs that have to be done as a new building takes shape. Foundations must be dug to support the walls. When that's done, bricks or concrete blocks can be put in place. Windows and a roof are needed next. Inside, carpenters make floors and put in doors.

Electricians connect up lights and plugs, and plumbers make sure the kitchen and bathroom have water.

If the road is dug up you can peep into the complicated world that lies beneath your feet. Bundles of cables bring electricity to and from the power station to your street, and wires from all the homes are linked to them.

Underground telephone wires can connect you to millions of other telephones many miles away. Water is piped from big water mains to every building and waste water from your drainpipes goes to the sewer under the road to be carried away.

Make

Make a map or model of your area. Put in old buildings, new houses, parks and roads. Try to find out how many people live in your town.

What a lot of people there must be in a big city. All the more friends for you, I suppose, and all the more jobs to choose from.

Socrates investigates

Draw

Draw a building site. Find pictures of diggers, dumpers and cranes to copy.

Where do I fit in?

> I'm a cat. I shall live here all my life and always do the same things. But what will you do when you grow up? Where will you live and what work would you like to do?

As you grow up you will leave your school and move on to another school or college. You will be able to go to new places, make new friends and try new things.

Most people look for a job when they leave school. They may move to a new home and have a family of their own.
Not everyone goes out to work. Some people stay at home looking after children or working for themselves.

Others can't go out to work because they are ill or because there are not enough jobs for everyone. It's very hard for people who want to work but can't find jobs, especially if they have families to care for.
It's fun to find out what other people do and imagine what you might be in the future. There is a place in the community for everyone.

Socrates investigates

Draw
Draw a picture to show what you think the factories and homes of the future will look like.

28

Talk

Talk to your friends about what you would like to be. Would you like to be a teacher with lots of people around you or would you prefer to be a train driver and work alone?

Note it down
How many jobs are mentioned in this book? Go back and see how many you can find.

> Very interesting! But all that talk of people and hard work makes me want a little nap. Goodbye!

INDEX